Dear Parent:

Congratulations! Your child is taking
the first steps on an exciting journey.
The destination? Independent reading!

STEP INTO READING® will help your c   s
five steps to reading success. Each step includes fun stories and colorful art.
There are also Step into Reading Sticker Books, Step into Reading Math
Readers, Step into Reading Write-In Readers, Step into Reading Phonics
Readers, and Step into Reading Phonics First Steps! Boxed Sets—a complete
literacy program with something for every child.

Learning to Read, Step by Step!

Ready to Read   Preschool–Kindergarten
• big type and easy words • rhyme and rhythm • picture clues
For children who know the alphabet and are eager to
begin reading.

Reading with Help   Preschool–Grade 1
• basic vocabulary • short sentences • simple stories
For children who recognize familiar words and sound out
new words with help.

Reading on Your Own   Grades 1–3
• engaging characters • easy-to-follow plots • popular topics
For children who are ready to read on their own.

Reading Paragraphs   Grades 2–3
• challenging vocabulary • short paragraphs • exciting stories
For newly independent readers who read simple sentences
with confidence.

Ready for Chapters   Grades 2–4
• chapters • longer paragraphs • full-color art
For children who want to take the plunge into chapter books
but still like colorful pictures.

STEP INTO READING® is designed to give every child a successful
reading experience. The grade levels are only guides. Children can progress
through the steps at their own speed, developing confidence in their
reading, no matter what their grade.

Remember, a lifetime love of reading starts with a single step!

For Theresa and the Prochazka clan
—S.R.R.

For Pop
—J.M.

Portraits of Lewis and Clark by Charles Willson Peale courtesy of
Independence National Historical Park.
Text copyright © 2003 by Shirley Raye Redmond.
Illustrations copyright © 2003 by John Manders.
All rights reserved under International and Pan-American Copyright Conventions.
Published in the United States by Random House Children's Books,
a division of Random House, Inc., New York, and simultaneously in
Canada by Random House of Canada Limited, Toronto.

www.stepintoreading.com
Educators and librarians, for a variety of teaching tools, visit us at
www.randomhouse.com/teachers

Library of Congress Cataloging-in-Publication Data
Redmond, Shirley Raye.
Lewis and Clark : a prairie dog for the president / by Shirley Raye Redmond ; illustrated
by John Manders. p. cm. — (Step into reading. A step 3 book.) SUMMARY: Introduces
Meriwether Lewis and William Clark, who, during their exploration of the West for
Thomas Jefferson, captured a prairie dog and sent it to the president as a gift.
ISBN 0-375-81120-6 (trade) — ISBN 0-375-91120-0 (lib. bdg.) 1. Lewis and Clark
Expedition (1804–1806)—Juvenile literature. 2. Lewis, Meriwether, 1774–1809—Juvenile
literature. 3. Clark, William, 1770–1838—Juvenile literature. 4. Jefferson, Thomas,
1743–1826—Juvenile literature. 5. West (U.S.)—Description and travel—Juvenile
literature. 6. West (U.S.)—Discovery and exploration—Juvenile literature. 7. Prairie
dogs—West (U.S.)—Anecdotes—Juvenile literature. [1. Lewis and Clark Expedition
(1804–1806) 2. Lewis, Meriwether, 1774–1809. 3. Clark, William, 1770–1838. 4. Jefferson,
Thomas, 1743–1826. 5. Prairie dogs. 6. Explorers. 7. West (U.S.)—Discovery and
exploration.] I. Manders, John, ill. II. Title. III. Step into reading.
Step 3 book. F592.7 .R43 2003 917.804'2—dc21 2002017829

Printed in the United States of America 10 9 8   First Edition

STEP INTO READING, RANDOM HOUSE, and the Random House colophon are registered
trademarks of Random House, Inc.

STEP INTO READING®

STEP 3

Lewis and Clark

A Prairie Dog for the President

by Shirley Raye Redmond
illustrated by John Manders

Random House 🏠 New York

In 1803, Thomas Jefferson
was the president
of the United States.

The country was still new.

It was also *very* big!

It was so big no one

had ever explored it all.

President Jefferson wondered

how long it would take

to reach the Pacific Ocean.

He wondered what the land

was like along the way.

The president wrote to his
friend Meriwether Lewis.

Lewis was a soldier.

He wanted to be an explorer.

Lewis's buddy William Clark

wanted to be an explorer too.

Lewis and Clark

went to see the president.

"I need someone

to explore the West,"

said the president.

"We'll do it!"

said Lewis and Clark.

The president told
Lewis and Clark
to make maps
and explore rivers.
He told them to collect plants
and draw wild animals.
Most important,
he told them to send presents!

Lewis and Clark
needed helpers for
their journey.

They took soldiers,

scouts, and boatmen.

Lewis even took his dog.

It was a *long* trip.
One of the scouts
brought his wife,
Sacagawea
(sack-uh-juh-WEE-uh).
Sacagawea was a big help.
She picked nuts and berries.

She cooked meat and stew.

She talked and traded
with the Indians
they met on the way.

Out west,

Lewis and Clark made maps.

They explored rivers.

They collected plants.

They saw animals

they had never seen before.

They saw buffalo.

They saw grizzly bears.

buffalo

They saw jackrabbits
with long ears.
They drew pictures
of the animals.

jackrabbit
with long ears

grizzly
bear

They tried to catch
some of the animals
to send to the president.

But the buffalo were too big.

The grizzly bears
were too dangerous.

The jackrabbits

were too fast.

"The president will think

we've forgotten him,"

they worried.

One day, Lewis and Clark

came to a prairie.

The ground was

filled with holes.

A little animal sat

by each hole.

"What are those?" asked Lewis.

Just then

a hawk flew overhead.

The little animals barked.

Then they dived

into their holes.

"Let's catch one of
those rascals," Clark said.
"They are small enough
to send to the president."

The soldiers
took shovels and picks.
They dug and dug.
But the little animals
were too fast.

"Let's flood them out,"
Lewis said.
The men carried water
from the river.

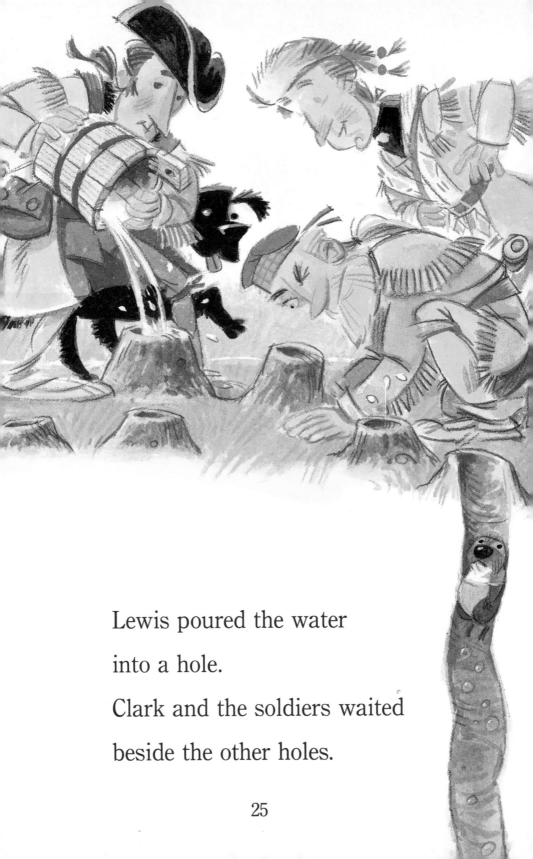

Lewis poured the water
into a hole.
Clark and the soldiers waited
beside the other holes.

They waited

and waited

and waited.

Then one of the animals
popped up.
"I've got it!" said Clark.

Clark put the animal in a cage.

"I wonder what it is?" he said.

Lewis laughed,

"It is a wet rodent!

You can call it a ground rat."

"No," said Clark.

"It looks like a squirrel.

I'll call it a barking squirrel."

"Squirrels don't bark,"
said a soldier.
"Dogs bark.
We should call it
a prairie dog."
"That's it!"
Lewis and Clark agreed.

Lewis and Clark

picked a scout to take

the prairie dog

to the president.

Clark also gave the scout

some birds to take.

They were called magpies.

Lewis gave the scout a letter

for the president.

He gave him plants
that he had collected.
The soldiers gave him
buffalo skins and deer horns.
"Have a nice trip!"
said Lewis and Clark.

31

The scout and the animals

rode a barge down the river.

They boarded a big ship
in New Orleans.

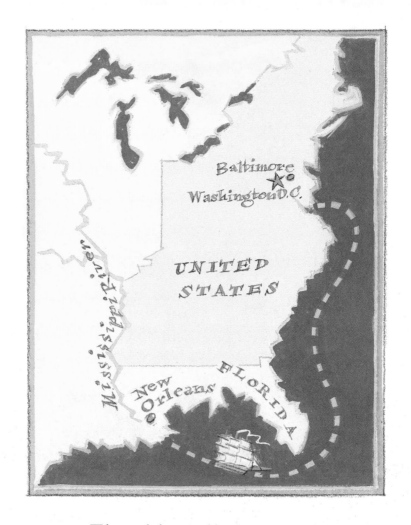

The ship sailed
around Florida.
Then it sailed north
to Baltimore, Maryland.
Finally, the ship
landed in Baltimore.

The scout put the animals

and the other presents

into the back of a wagon.

He paid the driver

to take everything

to President Jefferson

in Washington, D.C.

The president met the wagon

at the White House.

He picked up

the prairie dog's cage.

"Is this a gopher?" he asked.

"No," said the driver.

"I think it is a woodchuck."

President Jefferson
read the letter from Lewis.
"A soldier named this creature
a prairie dog.
It lives on the Western prairie
and barks like a dog."

The president gave
the prairie dog
a piece of apple.
Chomp!
The prairie dog
gobbled it right up.

The president laughed.
"Americans will want to see
this little fellow," he said.
"I will send these fine presents
to Mr. Peale's museum."

Mr. Peale's museum

was in Philadelphia.

The prairie dog

and the other gifts

rode in a stagecoach

to the museum.

It was a very bumpy ride.

Mr. Peale loved the presents.

He sent President Jefferson

a thank-you note.

"The prairie dog is

a pleasing little animal.

He is not at all dangerous

like a groundhog," he wrote.

Mr. Peale put the cage
in a sunny room.
Children came
to see the prairie dog.
Artists came
to draw its picture.

The visitors touched
the buffalo skins
and the deer horns.
They stared at the magpies.
"The American West must be
a wonderful place," they said.

The West *was* wonderful.

Lewis and Clark were gone

for two years exploring it.

In November of 1805,

they finally reached

the Pacific Ocean.

They were heroes.

If you travel west today,
you can still see
some of the sights
Lewis and Clark saw.
You can see
grizzly bears and buffalo.
You can see
jackrabbits and magpies.
And if you are lucky,
you might even see
a prairie dog!

Meriwether Lewis　　**William Clark**

Author's Note:

This is a true story,

and Lewis and Clark

were real explorers.

Mr. Peale was also an artist.

He painted these pictures

of Lewis and Clark

and put them in his museum.

Today the museum

is called Independence Hall.